This Is My Body

SERIES EDITORS

Chris Abani & Susannah Young-ah Gottlieb

This Is My Body

Poems

Jonathan Fletcher

NORTHWESTERN UNIVERSITY PRESS

EVANSTON, ILLINOIS

Northwestern University Press
www.nupress.northwestern.edu

Northwestern University Poetry and Poetics Colloquium
www.poetry.northwestern.edu

Printed in the United States of America

10 9 8 7 6 5 4 3 2 1

Library of Congress Cataloging-in-Publication Data
Names: Fletcher, Jonathan M., author.
Title: This is my body : poems / Jonathan Fletcher.
Other titles: This is my body (Compilation)
Description: Evanston, Illinois : Northwestern University Press, 2025. |
Series: Drinking gourd chapbook poetry prize
Identifiers: LCCN 2024028614 | ISBN 9780810148253 (paperback) |
ISBN 9780810148260 (ebook)
Subjects: LCGFT: Poetry.
Classification: LCC PS3556.L516 T48 2025 | DDC 811/.54—dc23/eng/20240708
LC record available at https://lccn.loc.gov/2024028614

for my mother

Contents

Foreword

Chris Abani and Susannah Young-ah Gottlieb

In an era marked by frequent, almost habitual experimentation in form and content, *This Is My Body* is an unexpected return to unadorned engagement. The engagements here are not erasures, redactions, or historical postulations; nor do they succumb to the precious anxieties of personal identity. We encounter a human voice as it explores yearning, loss, trepidation, love, and invisibility in an unvarnished approach that is as elegant as it is unpretentious. At the center of the book is a body constructed of desire and melancholy, a coming into being, the negotiation of a complicated and ever-shifting self—all offered up to the reader in an enactment like the Eucharist: a reaching not only for the ineffable but a hope for embodied redemption.

We enter the collection with "Jonathan" and feel the innocent humanity of friendship, the way nascent masculinities try with the limited tools given to construct a genuine tenderness. But the guileless honesty of affection between two young men rapidly evolves into an intimacy that threatens the comfort of one of their fathers. Here, as elsewhere throughout the collection, we discern a certain Adamic rebellion and the luminous, felt presence of deity. The language is highly biblical—not in the direct way of worship and belief, but in the way of rebellion, of pushing against a patriarchy too constrictive even for the masculinity seeking expression here.

The directness of Fletcher's language is intimate and visceral, but carefully crafted, so that the feeling of intimacy isn't that of reading someone's journal, but of being a close and confidential observer: over the shoulder, and—sometimes, it feels—inside their head. The struggles are not strictly circumscribed by sexuality, desire, and identity, but embrace the ways in which race, skin, ethnicity, and even the outsider position of nerd complicate the central provocations. The quest is to be seen, perhaps in the way that John Berger talks about seeing as a vital witness to existence. The weave of the speaker's self—the warp of race, the weft of identities—sometimes smoothed out by the lover who claims not to see these things, to see only a pure self, exacerbates the feeling of being erased. The earnestness of the voice, the lack of obfuscation in ornamentation and conceit, can make the work feel nakedly intense and overwhelming at times. And that is perhaps the greatest achievement of the collection: we replace the speaker's unadorned body with our own, newly bare, rebellious, and blessed.

Jonathan

2 Samuel 1:26

Though I did not call you
David, you were my David.

Though you called me Jonathan,
I wasn't an archer. I wasn't a singer.
I wasn't the son of a king.

Though disliked by your philistine
of a father, I refused to stay away.
When allowed to your house
no more, I invited you to mine.

As we bathed together,
compared bodies—mine brown
and foreskinned, yours light
and circumcised—we wondered
whose was better, cleaner.

Though we dried together,
changed together, snuggled
with action figures
together, your father was
wrong about us.
Even Saul couldn't have kept us apart.

Dirigibles

In high school, I was a nobody,
but was big, a blimp.
And the bullies teased me
for my size, called me
Goodyear in the halls

I tried to rise above them,
but they still dragged
me down. My hope
deflated. Then I met you

Like me, you were big
—a zeppelin, in fact—
but you loved yourself,
your body no less

To my surprise,
you even loved mine,
taught me to do the same

And like dirigibles,
we lifted off, rose
above the crowd

As we got higher,
they grew smaller

And we glided—
graceful crafts
carried by heat

Killing Crockett

When still a child, John Wayne
my idol, I'd fight you regularly,

Until one of us surrendered,
I'd refuse to change into pajamas,
insisted on wearing to bed
my Davy Crockett outfit:
a well-worn coonskin cap,
buckskin vest and pants.

I even turned our den into a fort:
chairs, cushions, and blankets
for limestone, wood, and mud.

With my belly on the carpet,
popgun in hand—cocked,
aimed at an imaginary,
parti-colored army—I'd cry
Remember the Alamo!

I cried, too, when the other boys,
sticks in hand—wielded
like bowie knives—drew a line
in the pea gravel, blocked
the playset entrance at recess:

Santa Anna's not allowed on the Alamo.

Your kind killed the King of the Wild Frontier!

Wounded by their words,
I rubbed my eyes,
red and swollen,
wide in realization:
I am darker than buckskin.

Stigmata

The marks across my wrists are
not miraculous.

Long sleeves help hide them.
I never show them.
Who'd want to see them?

Neither caressed nor kissed,
notched with scars, too,
my skin speaks,
tells what a red Victorinox
can do with time.

How like a cross is a pocketknife!

Though assured the Lord knows
my pain, I'm doubtful.

Like Thomas,
I need to touch the holes
of the risen Christ,
feel where nail crushed bone,
water and blood
pumped through punctures.

I'll believe it when I finger His wounds;
then I want Him to feel mine.

Near-Death Experience

I encountered no bright light, except
for the blinding ovals in the ceiling
of the blaring ambulance. Or
the end of a pen-shaped flashlight,
pointed at my pupils by a gloved hand.
Can you tell me your name?

I moved down no long tunnel, unless
you count the identical, sterile-white
halls. "Emergency Room" in bold,
bright red. I met no beings of light,
unless you count the white-coated
figures who rolled me in the gurney.

I felt no sense of peace, except
from the voices above me: *Stay with us,
Jonathan; you're still needed here.*
I was shown no life review, yet still questioned
my choices that led to this: a stomach
pump, earth-flavored charcoal.

I was greeted by no deceased family;
instead the family I still had, loved.
Surprised, touched by the flowers,
cards, balloons, we clasped hands
in my hospital room. Then wept
and prayed. And lived. And lived.

Coconut

Though hurled at me as a slur,
I like the taste of the fruit,
make from it cakes, cookies, milk, cheese.
I even rub its oil into my skin.
But it never lightens me for good.

When spoken to in Spanish,
I try to respond in kind.
But my vowels are as American
as apple pie. No one, though,
calls me "apple pie."

Had I gotten to shoot my roots
in the Global South,
flower in a family as dark as me,
would I be able to roll my r's?
I have the tongue, just not the mother.

Sometimes I'll kneel,
clench my hands, entreat a God
whom I'm sure is fair,
at least in skin,
though am not certain exists.

With fervent prayers,
interlaced fingers,
my knuckles whiten;
the rest of me doesn't.
O, perdóname, mi gente!
I don't deserve to be brown.

Velcro

Though nearly thirty,
inside your bedroom,
I turn back into a six-year-old.

You sit on the edge,
jacket off, blouse unbuttoned.
It has Velcro in the back.

I'm still afraid of the dark.
I need a night-light,
my mother's pats on my back,
before I can fall asleep.

I ask you to leave the lights bright.
With annoyance in your sigh,
you dim the room,
when you obviously want
to blacken it. *Dammit, Jonathan;
we're not here to sleep!*

Gently biting your bottom lip,
you guide the slider
of your zipper along its teeth,
where brass meets denim.
Must they be called teeth?

Friction is fun, unzipping
sexy, supposedly.
But I want my Teddy Ruxpin.
He's a bear. Fuzzy,
too, and warm.
His vest even has Velcro.

We used to cuddle in bed.
My mother never liked him,
threw him out
when he began to fray, smell.

With jeans now down to your socks,
you unhook your bra, slide off
your panties. Black lace
lands on my leather loafers.
Why do I feel more naked than you?

Mouth slightly creased into a smile,
clothes wrinkled, you sit atop
sheets yearning to be crumpled.

As you pat the bed, I try to guess
your brand of pants. Levi's? H&M?
Old Navy? Does that matter? Yes!

Though I know I shouldn't think
about other women now,
I can't stop seeing the shadow
of my mother, flashlight in hand,
checking for monsters
in my closet, below my bed.

But later, the hinges of my door
would creak, the coils of my mattress
squeak. What noises are scarier?
Before tonight,
I'd never felt so frightened.

Dr. Bailey

Every time we meet,
I share my secrets,
but you won't, can't
divulge yours to me.

Tell me about your mood,
sleep, appetite, stress,
your fears, hopes, plans, dreams.

Let me record them in my notes.
Let me write you refills for your meds.
Let's plan to talk
in three months.

Instead, you ask the questions.
Instead, you get to know me
through evaluations, assessments,
classifications in the *DSM*.

Instead, you adjust my milligrams,
track, mark my progress,
regress.
Instead, you scribble away
in your notepad.

In my journal,
I've done the same:

If you can diagnose me,
then cure me.
If you can't,
then love me.

Porcelain Mother

As a child, I wished to look like you,
asked the light-toned Lord to whiten me.
But the same God who molded
an earthen Adam didn't.

Or couldn't. Perhaps the Potter
can't make porcelain
without kaolin. Did he dig me
from the wrong color clay?

You assured me there were families
like us: mothers as light as chalk,
children dark as mud.
Materials that stain as easily as love.

To turn out the same hue as you,
I'd have gladly burned in a kiln.
But not all clay, however
baked, is meant to be china.

When reminded of the biblical verse,
*Dust thou art and unto dust
shalt thou return*, I only felt like dirt.

Mummy

Encased like a frozen Incan
mummy, I lie inside
a warm, plastic incubator,
a knitted cap atop my head,
a quilt around my body.

Lighter-skinned than the woman
who birthed me, you say
my name and smile, reach gently
into the ports, caress
my tubed, wired limbs.

Soon, they'll unhook me.
Soon, you'll hold me. Someday,
you'll tell me how you found
me, why you chose me,
what you sacrificed. And

layer by layer, layer by layer,
we'll unearth, unwrap,
reconstruct what we can.
And honor what has been lost.
And cradle what remains.

This Is My Body

this is my body

it will be given for none

this is my body

it won't be fixed or pitied

it won't be disrespected

it won't be tokenized

this is my body

it won't be fetishized

it won't be exoticized

it won't be infantilized

this is my body

it won't be mollified

it won't be interrogated

it will be recognized

this is my body

it will be validated

it will be incorporated

it will be accommodated

this is my body

it will be verbalized

it will be sacralized

it will be stroked and kissed

it will be felt and known

this is my body

remember this for me

Dinocampus coccinellae

Thanks to a virus
that attacks the brain—
much like the disease in mine—
you feast and grow
inside a ladybug, burst
from her abdomen.

Remarkably, she doesn't die.

As you weave a cocoon
between her legs, take
neurological control,
her spotted carapace of red
convulses, scaring
off potential predators.

It is possible she will recover,
only to be parasitized again.
It is possible she won't survive.

Maybe she'll unfold
her alae, flap
gently, then quickly,
trying to forget what resided
inside her head.

Medusa

The way you attach
electrodes to my scalp,
let them drape behind
my head, I must
look like a Gorgon.

Though punished
by no goddess, I feel
cursed. Though not quite
a Hippocrates, you diagnose,
treat. Though no oracle,
you foresee recovery:

Within six to eight sessions,
you should begin to feel
changes in your mood.

I want to believe
your prophecy.
I want to cut
back on Abilify,
Lamictal.

I want to kill
the monster inside.

But everywhere I look,
I see stone. I see gray.

Even the computer
you have me watch.
Even the bright,

colorful, looping
images. Even your face
in the monitor.
Even my own reflection.

WWJD (What Would Jonathan Do)

As frayed as my faith,
in fashion no more, my old
woven wristband reminds
me to do as Jesus would.

Though I no longer listen,
I cannot unfasten the article
that often chafes my skin.
Is it God who stops me?

Why, then, was it easy
to let go of the others:
unclasp my cross, slide
off my promise ring?

No more JOHN 3:16,
TRUE LOVE WAITS.
No more Bible studies,
no Cru or FCA.

With a bare neck, finger,
I leaf through the Good
Book. For the history,
literature, yet nothing else.

Still it sits on my shelf,
between *Atlas Shrugged*,
Thus Spake Zarathustra.
Pages wrinkled, margins full.

What I sometimes miss,
I fill
with knowledge now,
experience.

Self-Portrait as Whiter, Happier

Even with much time, work, progress,
I often see a stranger in the reflective glass.

Like mine, his hair is mostly straight,
parts on the right, curls around the ears.

But his locks are blond, eyes light, skin
fair. He wears a smile. And a suit and tie.

I want his complexion. I want his hair
and hue. I want the life that comes with it.

Short of that, let the world see me, itself
from different angles, with different light.

Let's reflect. Let's alter the image, the way
it's seen. Or, better yet, let's fracture it.

Marble

When I admitted
that I could go
no farther with you,
I thought, hoped you
might admire me.
Instead, you told me
that I must be stone.

What could I do
but watch you leave
like a patron exiting
a gallery, ignoring
the famous sculpture
of an armed, naked
Roman warrior.

How could I feel
anything but punished,
laid as bare to you
as a nude statue—
the head, arms, penis
missing—each victim
to age, neglect, weather.

Phineas Gage

At twenty-five, you lost a chunk of brain.
At twenty-five, mine changed irrevocably.

You weren't the same since.
I haven't been, either.

I'm still luckier than you,
nicer than the man you became.
But sometimes irritable, too.

Iron never punched through my skull,
carved out a slice of frontal lobe.
I didn't vomit up brain and blood.
The public never called me a miracle.

At circuses and carnivals,
you posed with the tamping rod
from your accident,
as though it were an artifact,
all to profit from your injury.
We do what we need to survive.

Meet Me Not in the Seventh Circle

If not for the thorns, gnarls,
sap for blood, the claws of Harpies,
I wouldn't mind turning into a tree.
Hell's only one form of punishment.
Sometimes medication doesn't help.
Sometimes my therapist makes
no sense. Sometimes I lie to him.
Yet it all now seems banal to me.
I'm in no hurry to descend.
There might be a chance I'll be saved,
separated from heathen relatives, friends.
I then remember there's always lust.
There's always greed, gluttony.

Horsemen of the Apocalypse

More than four in number—
181, in fact—you sailed
to the home of my ancestors,
anchored your caravels at Tumbes,
unloaded lances, falchions,
arquebuses, barbs,
jennets, Andalusians.

Though no gods yourselves,
you behaved like the one
from your Scriptures—
expected, demanded
offerings, more offerings.

To appease you, my ancestors
gifted you gold,
silver, emeralds, textiles
made of vicuña,
baskets stuffed with huaco.

To see your intentions, visions,
my ancestors needed
no book of Revelation:
brown necks, wrists, ankles
shackled, backs bent,
pustuled, blistered red—
smallpox, whips to blame.

As unwelcome as what
you brought: war, conquest,
disease, famine,
your arrival opened up
a new world—one
you blessed and filled
atop the ruins of an Other.

Evolution of an Organism

1984: I am born and adopted.

1996: DOMA is passed.

1997: I boycott Ellen DeGeneres.

1998: Matthew Shepard is murdered.

2000: I meet my first openly gay teacher.

2003: Supreme Court rules on *Lawrence v. Texas*.

2003: I vote for Bush.

2004: Massachusetts legalizes same-sex marriage.

2007: My best friend comes out to me.

2008: California achieves marriage equality.

2008: My supervisor comes out.

2008: California passes Prop 8.

2009: I visit my first gay bar.

2011: "Don't Ask, Don't Tell" is repealed.

2014: I attend my first Pride parade.

2015: Gay marriage is legalized.

2022: I come out to my mom.

Scales

In a world of two,
I was one,
slithering slowly along.

Like the serpent in the Garden,
I wove through couples
of every color, arrangement:

Adams and Eves,
Eves and Eves,
Adams and Adams.

Helpmate to no one,
I felt sinful.
What was wrong with me?

I needed to know.
But there was no Tree of Knowledge,
only knowledge.

My first time with someone,
I felt dirty. Each
successive time, worse.

Though scaled in guilt,
I curled myself, again and again,
into others' expectations:

nibbling skin,
sucking juice, pretending
to like the taste of fruit,

while only wanting
to spit it out,
like bitter seeds.

Boys

Before there were girls, there was He-Man,
the X-Men, you, us. You always had

the bigger collection; I, more imagination:
Let's use your mom's yarn; let's string

a zipline so our guys can fly! The best part
of sleepover: pretend-play in your bathtub.

Pew-pew! Pew-pew! You can't get me,
Skeletor! Soapsuds made the best defense.

Pew-pew! Pew-pew! Hit me if you can,
Magneto! By the time your mom called us,

our hair was dry, our fingers prunes,
the water cool. *Ten more minutes, please!*

We'd get five. Then time for bed. *PJs,*
now! You'd take Wolverine; I, He-Man.

Nothing's better than a power sword!
Nuh-uh, claws are so much cooler!

The sheets pulled over us, you'd hug
to yourself your gloved, masked mutant;

I, my blond, breastplated barbarian.
Lights off now, misters! In only nightlight,

though, we'd whisper still, doing our best
to fool your mom, trying to keep one

another awake, too. Our heads atop
your X-Men pillows, our bodies beneath

your matching comforter, we'd fall asleep,
warm and peaceful, in one another's arms.

Acknowledgments

Thank you to the following publications, where some of these poems first appeared:

Big City Lit: "Velcro" (as "Unzipped")

Catch the Next: The Journal of Pedagogy and Creativity: "Killing Crockett"

Emerge Literary Journal: "Near-Death Experience"

Half Hour to Kill: "Dr. Bailey" (as "Patient")

MONO.: "Scales"

Moot Point Magazine: "Boys"

Otherwise Engaged: Literature and Arts Journal: "Phineas Gage"

New Feathers Anthology: "Coconut"

riverSedge: A Journal of Art and Literature: "Meet Me Not in the Seventh Circle"

Speakeasy: "*Dinocampus coccinellae*," "Medusa," "Mummy"

The Thing Itself: "Dirigibles"

Waco WordFest: "Porcelain Mother"

Special thanks to my professors and classmates at Columbia University School of the Arts, especially Finn Anderson, Latif Ba, Leia K. Bradley, Timothy Donnelly, Loisa Fenichell, Alan Gilbert, Dorothea Lasky, Shane McCrae, Deborah Paredez, Alex Romero, Joel Sedano, Emily Skillings, Ariel Joy So, and Tiffany Troy.

To my mentors, friends, and fellow writers, especially Matt Ahanni, Jacob Appel, José Angel Araguz, Dario Beniquez, Sheila Black, Richie

Hoffman, Alexandra van de Kamp, Katherine McDaniel, Leslie McIntosh, Emmy Pérez, Octavio Quintanilla, jo reyes-boitel, Alex Z. Salinas, and Vijay Seshadri.

To the San Antonio literary communities of which I am part, especially Gemini Ink and the San Antonio Writers' Guild.

To my fellow Zoeglossia Fellows.

To Chris Abani and Susannah Young-ah Gottlieb, and to Elena Bellaart, Anne Gendler, Marisa Emily Siegel, Courtney Smotherman, and the rest of the editorial team at Northwestern University Press, without whom this chapbook would not be a reality.

Finally, to my family for their unceasing support and encouragement, particularly my mother. This belongs to you.